O.L.D.
The Other Life Department.

By

Terence F Moss

Other works by the author.

Stage Musicals
Angels and Kings
Soul Traders

Pilot TV Comedy's
The Inglish Civil War
Closing Time

Novels
The Prospect of Redemption 2012
The Killing Plan 2013
The Tusitala 2015
Be Happy with my Life 2017

Stage Plays & Adaptations
Better by Far 2018
Petroleum 2021

Terence F. Moss
butchmoss@outlook.com
Terence F. Moss on Facebook

A comedy-drama with songs

This play presupposes that the Beatles never became famous and that they broke up in 1963.

The set is John's Lennon's, 3rd floor flat in Croydon, Surrey, in 2011.

The lounge is spacious, and in one corner is a mini grand piano. In the middle are two large sofa's and to one side there is an Ikea table and two chairs. On the other side is a peculiar piece of art resembling a chair. There are a large number of original paintings, objet d'art on plinths and the room is lined with bookcases filled with books. There are a couple of guitars and a ukulele in stands. There is a well-worn traditional partner oak desk with two computer laptops, piles of papers-books, etc. There are many photograph frames on the piano, a whiskey glass, and a Jack Daniels bottle.

There is a small kitchenette area off to one side and a couple of doors off the lounge, one to the bedroom and the bathroom. John is sitting at his piano as the scene opens. The room is predominantly white.

Character background.
John
John is in his seventies, overweight with a bohemian/hippy appearance about him, and he appears tired. He is suffering from early-onset dementia. He wears a patterned flower shirt and a black waistcoat undone. The hair at the back of his head is long and tied in a pigtail, trailing halfway down his back. The hair on the top of his head has receded considerably, with just tufts of hair sticking upwards. What little is left is sticking up a couple of inches as if it has been lacquered in a sort of semi Mohican style. He is wearing a pair of large horn-rimmed spectacles and smoking a marijuana joint which he places in an ashtray. He has a caustic temperament and occasionally drifts off into periods of deep melancholia.

George is in his late 60's. Thin, still has all his hair tied in a knot at the back of his head. He has a gentle, non-aggressive disposition and exudes a peaceful karma.

Lucy Lennon (John's daughter with Cynthia) is 44.

Cynthia Lennon late 60's (John's wife, she is dead) Forgiving.

Yoni 53 John's cleaner, Chinese or Japanese. Pragmatic.

John and George both have faint traces of a Liverpudlian accent.
The scene opens with the Beatles song "In My Life" playing.

"In My Life" fades away, and John starts to pick out a not immediately recognisable melody that segues into "In My Life."

SCENE ONE.

Day 1. 4-30pm
George arrives

John gets up from the piano and sits down at his desk, staring at a photograph in a silver frame. He picks the picture up - kisses it, and places it back down again. Then lights up his joint again, takes a couple of tokes, then stands up and moves across the room to his sofa. He sits down and picks up a TV remote control. He points at the giant screen on the wall, presses the remote three times, and a "broadband disconnected" error message appears.

He doesn't seem to notice this and settles back on the sofa and stares at the screen as if he can see something. He places the joint in an ashtray. After a minute, the doorbell buzz's, but he takes no notice. He picks up the joint – takes another toke - the doorbell rings again.
John stands up and wanders slowly across to the front door to open it; he pauses at the piano to look at the photographs. The joint is still in his hand. The constant ringing of the doorbell does not prompt John to move any faster.

George is dressed in a SKY engineers uniform and is carrying a small box of tools and a Skybox under his arm; he is reading from some notes on a clipboard which he is holding in his other hand. George is thin, taller than John, with a thick, lustrous head of hair cut in the style of a much younger man, and he has a goatee beard. He is sixty-seven years old but appears more youthful.

JOHN

John opens the front door and takes a toke on his joint.
Yes!
He fires the word abruptly, letting the smoke slowly exhale through his mouth.

GEORGE

He looks up at John and smiles. George has a cheerful disposition.
Sorry, I'm a bit late.

JOHN

Are you?

GEORGE

Yes. I've been ringing your bell for ages. I thought maybe you weren't in. I was just about to go.
George smiles again, this time with an even broader, slightly demented grin.

JOHN

Expressionless
Were you?

GEORGE

Yes.

JOHN

Well, I am.

GEORGE

What?

JOHN

In.

GEORGE

Yes. I can see that.

JOHN

John pauses for a moment to catch up.
You rang the bell?

GEORGE

That's right.

George looks a little confused and checks his clipboard
Mr Lemon, isn't it?
He asks this with a quizzical expression as if unsure.

John does not respond but glares at George.
JOHN

Nope.

GEORGE

No? Are you sure?

JOHN

Yes

GEORGE

Not Mr J. lemon?

JOHN

Nope.

GEORGE

Does a Mr Lemon live here with you?

JOHN

Nope.
John takes another toke on his joint.

GEORGE

Oh.
He looks perplexed.

JOHN

pauses…
Len…Non! the names Len…Non, not Lemon
Curtly enunciating the two syllables of his name as if talking to a child.

GEORGE

George pauses for a few seconds and flicks back through the paperwork he is holding. After a few moments, riffling through his notes and with some considerable reservation, he reluctantly replies.
Are you absolutely sure about that? It definitely says Mr Lemon here.

George taps his notes.

JOHN

Now a little stressed.
Does it?
He exhales some smoke slowly.

GEORGE

Recognises the aroma but reacts with moderation.
Yes.
George pauses for a few moments, unsure as to how he should proceed.
Have you changed your name recently?

JOHN

Nope. Why would I change my name to Lemon?

GEORGE

I don't know, must admit it is a bit odd. But I do come across some bizarre things in my job.
He smiles again.

JOHN

Do you?

GEORGE

Yes. Just the other day/

JOHN

John interrupts abruptly; he is now losing his patience.
/Why the fuck did you ring the bell?

GEORGE

George is slightly taken aback by John's abrupt question but continues.

I'm George, the service engineer. I've come to repair your Sky.

JOHN

John peers casually upwards as if looking for something.
Is it broken then?

GEORGE

I believe so.
He checks his clipboard

JOHN

John is still gazing skywards
Looks alright to me.

GEORGE

Not that sky…
George appears a little perplexed
your Sky television box. I'm the broadband engineer from Sky.
He annunciates this noticeably slower.

JOHN.

Are you now?

GEORGE

Yes.

George slowly points warily at his tool bag boldly emblazoned with the word SKY
He slowly lifts the bag, so John can clearly see the logo.

JOHN

Acknowledges the logo and smiles.
Sky!

GEORGE

George smiles moronically
Yes.

JOHN

beat
Do I look like a lemon…mate?
He heavily emphasises the last word.

GEORGE

George gazes at John for a few moments gauging his demeanour. He replies unhurriedly with a hint of playful mischief.
No… if pushed, I'd probably say … a coconut.

JOHN

John smiles.
A coconut… why a fucking coconut.
John appears insulted but contained.

GEORGE

I don't know. It's just the first thing that popped into my head.

JOHN

I find that a little disturbing. I'd get your head
looked at if I were you.

GEORGE

Maybe it's the hair? Yes, that must be it.

JOHN

Indignantly

What's wrong with my hair?

GEORGE

Nothing, nothing at all. It's a… it's unique,

beat

very special, very you, sir.

George smiles again.

JOHN

John muses contemplatively over George's comment.

But why a coconut? And you don't have to call
me, sir. I'm not a knight… yet.

*The last word is spoken animatedly in a flourish as if it is
imminently expected.*

GEORGE

Tongue in cheek

I don't know. Would it sound better if I said…
a very distinguished-looking coconut?

JOHN

No, it wouldn't sound any fucking better. You
would just sound like an obsequious little toad
taking the piss.

13

GEORGE

I do apologise Mr Lemon. I really didn't come here to antagonise you.

JOHN

Firmly

Lennon, it's fucking Lennon and take it from me; from where I'm standing, it sounds very much like you are taking the piss. First, you call me lemon, then add insult to injury by saying I look like a coconut. What would you make of it if someone said you looked like a bloody coconut?

GEORGE

I was just being candid.

JOHN

Candid! Well, it's only a coconut hair's breadth between candid and bloody offensive from where I'm standing.

GEORGE

Look! can we start again? It has been an awfully long and weary day.

JOHN

Aren't they all?... And getting longer and wearier by the minute at this rate.

GEORGE

I really didn't mean to cause offence, you know… it's just that…

George hesitates while assessing John's expression.

JOHN

John's expression of extreme indignation suddenly changes, and he smiles contritely, gesturing to George to come in.

It's alright. Forget it. No offence taken. I've had a pretty shitty day myself as it is.   Please forgive me, do come in.

He takes another toke.

GEORGE

George acknowledges the apology by nodding his head and making a small gesture with his hand. They both smile at each other in a half-hearted and slightly awkward manner. George enters and puts his tools and the sky box on the floor. George mutters.

No problem.

JOHN

So, George the Skyman, now we've got the introductions out of the way; why exactly are you here?

GEORGE

George holds up his SKY clipboard.

As I said, I've come to fix your telly. We had a call to say you had a problem with your sky box; apparently, it's not working.

George smiles Stan Laurel style.

JOHN

Surprised
> Isn't it? I didn't know that.

GEORGE

> So, is your television working at all?

JOHN

> I think so. I thought I was just watching Holidays in the Sun.

He appears a little confused.
> I think we're in Bognor Regis today. It looks shit.

GEORGE

> Well, that's odd, we had a call from…

George flicks through the papers on his clipboard and reluctantly continues…
> A Mrs Lemon… your wife?

JOHN

> Probably not… she's dead… died two years ago. So, unless she's managed to develop supernatural psychic powers, I'd say…

GEORGE

George interrupts. He is looking at his clipboard.
> It definitely says a Mrs Lucy Lemon made the call.

JOHN

Ahhh, Lucy, yes, she's my daughter. Come to think of it, I did mention it to her last night…

John does not overreact to the repeated mispronunciation issue this time. He appears to have temporarily come to terms with the problem, but his head twitches to one side as if he has some sort of affliction.

They always get the name wrong over the phone. This would never have happened if I'd been famous. Then they'd get it right.

GEORGE

Looking at the blank screen with a broadband error message

Your screen is blank. There's nothing there. Didn't you notice that?

JOHN

I thought that was still Bognor.

GEORGE

Have you got the control panel?

JOHN

Yes,

John picks it up and hands it to George.

GEORGE

George presses a few buttons while pointing it at the TV, but nothing happens.

It's buggered.

JOHN

Is it?

GEORGE

Yes.

JOHN

And that's a technical expression, is it?

GEORGE

What?

JOHN

Buggered!

GEORGE

Playing along

Oh yes, in the trade, that is.

JOHN

Oh.

GEORGE

I'll have to check it out.

JOHN

John flashes a sardonically knowing expression.

Oh, right.

GEORGE

beat

Are you then?

Sounding a little unsure.

JOHN

What?

GEORGE

Famous?

JOHN

Me? No! Why?

GEORGE

You said…

JOHN

No, what I meant was, if I "was" famous…
they wouldn't get my name… oh, never mind.
John emphasises the word "was."

GEORGE

Oh, I see.
beat
In a philosophical tone.
That's the rub, though, isn't it? The malevolent
paradox of obscurity.

JOHN

A little stunned by the remark.
What?

GEORGE

Fame.

JOHN

Sounds a little unsure
What about it?

GEORGE

It's the affliction of the internet, the endemic plague that haunts the proletariat masses.

JOHN

Does it? I hadn't noticed.

GEORGE

Insecurity… and the fear of obscurity, inflamed by the skulking threat of insignificance and lingering inconsequentiality. If you don't have a social media presence, you're nobody. You don't really exist. It's a brain disease.

JOHN

Is it? I didn't notice that either.

GEORGE

Oh yes. Those without it aspire to break free from the manacled chains of murky mundane anonymity and the yoke of irrelevance and subservience that it brings - but those with it…
– the famous ones, those that have a "presence" … well, they pray – maybe a little half-heartedly and not with any genuine sincerity for anonymity to return.

CONT……….

GEORGE CONT...

But they don't really want to be inconspicuous and ordinary and unrecognised like the rest of us. They just want to remain aloof and appear enigmatically conspicuous by their absence - fame by juxtaposition if you like.

Deep down, everybody wants to be legendary and immortal, but they also want to be a little mysterious.   ...It's the blight of our godless times, and it is critically important to understand the psyche of your friends and workmates, and that's what I try to do. I see this scourge of desire as the first stage of failure on the pathway to the civilised world's ultimate decline and fall.

JOHN

John is a little dazed by George's explication, so he takes another toke on his joint and waits for a few seconds...
Well, that's a jolly thought.

GEORGE

George doesn't appear to notice John's glib comment.
Oh yes. Everybody wants to be a celebrity these days, at almost any price. That's why reality TV shows populated by talentless morons are so popular. Virtually any level of degradation and humiliation will be endured in the pursuit of the cursed chalice. That's all they ever think about. A sip from the goblet of materialism, nothing else seems to matter anymore. It's all so pitifully desperate.

JOHN

Slightly bewildered
Is it?

GEORGE

Absolutely.

JOHN

Even at suppertime?

GEORGE

Suppertime?

JOHN

Do all these people want to be famous even at suppertime?

GEORGE

Well, yes, I suppose so.
He sounds mystified.

JOHN

Does that include you?

GEORGE

Brushes that aside with a flick of his hand.
Me no. I don't want to be famous.
George is still confused

JOHN

Good. I wouldn't want any sudden bid for international stardom to interrupt my dining arrangements.

GEORGE

George looks surprised at Johns retort
Dining arrangements?

JOHN

John takes another toke on his joint and offers it to George.
George declines with a shake of his head.
I was looking forward to my fish supper and Coronation street.

GEORGE

Were you... Oh, I see...
He pauses for a few seconds deliberating over what John has just said.
I like that; very droll.

JOHN

John appears confused.
What?

GEORGE

What you just did, very amusing and so wittily pertinent to our conversation.

JOHN

John appears further confused.
What did I do?

GEORGE

In essence, and I place the emphasis on the essence, I was endeavouring to articulate a profoundly existentialistic comment about the deteriorating state of the world, and the nihilistic obsession of so many of its inhabitants with fame, vacuous popularity and the mindless pursuit of an illusion, and you, with a few brief mutterings, managed to condense the pending demise of the social heritage of our planet as something of no meaningful significance so long as it doesn't interfere with your tea.

JOHN

Supper.

GEORGE

Supper then.

JOHN

Confused and glazing over.
Did I?

GEORGE

You did.

JOHN

Well, I'm sorry, but dinner is essential to me.

GEORGE

Supper?

JOHN

No, dinner, I have dinner at suppertime.

GEORGE

Oh, so when do you have dinner?

JOHN

Non-plussed,
Tea time, of course.

GEORGE

He looks a little confused.
John offers his joint to George, George declines but waveringly.
Now I see… I think.
They both say nothing for a few moments
The body is a tiny temple, you know, a living shrine of the soul.

JOHN

I think mine is leaning more towards a cathedral.
John smiles to himself as he glances down at his ample stomach.

George misses the joke and looks confused.
(Beat)…………..

GEORGE

The problem is your name and you being in Bangalore.

JOHN

John looks confused and pauses for a few seconds.
I thought this was Croydon?

GEORGE

No. You are in Croydon, but the call centre is in Bangalore, that's in India.

JOHN

Sharply
I know where Bangalore is.

GEORGE

Of course you do, I realise that, but not everybody does. You'd be surprised how many people think it's in North Wales.
When someone starts speaking with a Punjabi accent, they become baffled. They're expecting Rob Brydon, and they get Gandhi. Can't get their heads around that. Hence the cockup with your name. It's pretty normal.

JOHN

Is it?

GEORGE

Nodding his head profusely
Oh yes.

JOHN

You must have my account details somewhere. They must be correct.

GEORGE

Appearing a little reluctant to speak.
They may well have been,
George glances down at his clipboard again.
...but they've probably been updated by the computer looking at this.

JOHN

John answers with some growing concern...
Updated?

GEORGE

It happens occasionally, but I will make sure the name is changed... back to Lennon.

JOHN

Hmmm... right. Ta.

GEORGE

It's all state of the art now. Everything's done with artificial intelligence, super robots... smart appliances – it's all incredibly clever stuff.

JOHN

Is it...?
John sniffs
They got my name wrong!

George makes a conciliatory expression
GEORGE

Anyway, where's your router and where does the cable come in. Once I've sorted this out, I can go home for my tea.

JOHN

Oh right. Well, it's some sort of communal system. We just have the three outlets, one over there…

John points to a socket on the far wall.

One with the router, which I believe is in the TV cabinet, and one other in the bedroom.

GEORGE

Right. I'll get to work.

John gazes at George with a quizzical expression. He takes another toke on his spliff and wonders around the room, looking back at George from different angles while George is unscrewing the socket. George looks up at John, wondering what he's doing and gives him a half smile.

JOHN

Sorry, did you want a…?

He offers the joint to George.

GEORGE

Shakes his head.

You did ask me earlier, thank you, but I gave it up in the sixties.

JOHN

Good for you, mate… good for you.

GEORGE

You can call me George if you like?

JOHN

George, right. Yes, you did mention that earlier, didn't you?

GEORGE

I did.

JOHN

He holds up one finger and waves it at George, and winks an eye.

Right. I'll call you George in future.

George smiles

John pauses for a few seconds before gingerly asking...

Do I detect the relics of a scouse accent in there somewhere?

GEORGE

George stops what he's doing and sits down on the floor, looking up at John for a few moments.

Well, I bloody well hope so. We did go to the same school in Liverpool at the same time, and we were in the same band for a couple of years.

JOHN

You didn't mention that when you came in.

GEORGE

Well, I wasn't sure, to begin with, you have changed quite a bit...

George points at John's belly.

... and anyway, I didn't know if you would have remembered me. It was a long time ago, nearly fifty years. And I did have your name wrong.

JOHN

I knew there was something about you when you came in, just couldn't figure it out.

GEORGE

Probably the uniform; it does catch the eye.

JOHN

It's Hamilton, isn't it? George Hamilton, I clearly remember that much.

GEORGE

George smiles. He knows John is joshing with him.

Not that clearly, it's Harrison, George Harrison, not Hamilton.

.

JOHN

John laughs

Of course it is, just joshing.

(beat)

We're even now, aren't we?

John smirks.

GEORGE

Still smiles but is a little unsure.
Are we?

JOHN

John thinks for a few moments.
The Silver Beetles! That was the group we were in, the Silver fucking Beetles.

GEORGE

That's right, so you do remember?

JOHN

It's coming back to me slowly.

GEORGE

With pride.
We played nightclubs and strip joints in Germany back in 1960 and 61, do you remember that?

JOHN

Vaguely. Spent most of those days getting drunk; I remember that much.

GEORGE

We were there a long time with nothing to do to fill the days.

JOHN

There were a lot of whores... for that.

GEORGE

Gazes skyward, briefly reminiscing, then starts fiddly with the socket again.

Best years of my life.

JOHN

Best years of our lives. Shame it all went tits up after that.

GEORGE

Do you miss the band?

JOHN

I miss the playing... and the drinking.... And the shagging...

GEORGE

No real regrets, then?

JOHN

A few.

GEORGE

Like...?

JOHN

I still miss Stuart. We could have been a great band if he hadn't died. Do you remember Stuart?

GEORGE

Sort off. I remember the two of you were always fighting; I thought you hated each other.

JOHN

Not really, and we weren't really fighting.

GEORGE

Appears intrigued.

Weren't you? I always thought you despised him because he had a natural musical talent and always managed to pull the attractive women. You always got the rough old slags, as I recall?

George half-smiles at his putdown.

JOHN

Did I...? I don't remember.

GEORGE

I was a little in awe of him as well. Reminded me a bit of James Dean. I always thought he would become something, I don't know what but...

JOHN

He was hard to figure out at times

GEORGE

Enigmatic. Looking back, that's what I thought he was.

JOHN

Really?

GEORGE

Yes.

JOHN

Reflectively
Enigmatic?

GEORGE

Yes. There was something moody - unfamiliar about him. Maybe he was just simply destined to be famous?

JOHN

You think so?

GEORGE

I did, but then he died.
(Beat)

JOHN

So, I only got the rough old slags?

GEORGE

I remember that much, even now. Rough as arseholes, usually blonde, but they always had big...
He gestures large breasts

JOHN

Did they...
John wanders around the room again, musing for a few moments, taking a sip from a glass of whiskey on the piano, looking at the floor, looking up at George, and then back at the floor.

JOHN

Not like the rest of us then, destined for obscurity.

GEORGE

Sorry?

JOHN

Stuart. You think he would have been famous?

GEORGE

Had he lived, possibly, but he didn't, so it didn't happen.

JOHN

Yea, you do have to be alive to become famous.

GEORGE

Not necessarily, but it helps... if you want to enjoy it.

JOHN

Em... I didn't kill him, you know!

GEORGE

George stops fiddling with the socket and looks at John, a little astounded by his statement.
What?

JOHN

Stuart, I didn't kill him. The hospital said he had a brain haemorrhage.

GEORGE

I never thought you did. I'd almost forgotten all about that. What made you mention it?

JOHN

I don't know, something Pauli said years ago... it sort of stuck.

beat

He comes back to me from time to time, you know, like the ghost of Banquo...

GEORGE

Who?

JOHN

Stuart... I see him from time to time... he just sits in that chair and watches me.

John points to an Ikea chair. One of a pair.

JOHN

He said it was all my fault because I was constantly battering him.

GEORGE

What, Stuart?

JOHN

No, not Stuart, Pauli.

GEORGE

What little I do remember, and it isn't much, was we all battered the hell out of each other at one stage or another. Drink, drugs, no sleep, playing all night and fucking all day. There were always a few issues and a little friction.

(beat)

But you were always fighting with Stuart? I never understood that.

JOHN

John wanders around the room for a few moments before answering.

We weren't fighting, not really. I just needed to touch him - to smell him – to see him bleeding... I can't explain what it felt like having Stuart around. It was just... I don't know, a sort of primal sentience.

GEORGE

Primal sentience?

Not sure what John means.

JOHN

Wistfully

It's the difference between thinking something and feeling it... I could actually feel the life energy emanating from his body. It was overwhelming, overpowering at times... I felt I was drowning in who he was, sinking... disappearing from view and then... I needed to inhabit his existence to acquire his spirit... sort of...

GEORGE

Prosaically

He died.

JOHN

Brightly

Yep, but it really wasn't my fault... I loved him.

GEORGE

I never thought it was your fault.

JOHN

Pauli did.

Pauses to glance at George

He always said I killed him, that's why the band broke up, but he was wrong.

GEORGE

As I said, I don't remember that. I was a bit younger than you, more naïve, I suppose... still am as it happens. I missed all the hidden agendas back then, all the between the lines stuff. It was all black and white, as far as I recall.

JOHN

He always taunted me because I knocked Stuart out a few times, he said that's what caused the brain haemorrhage, but he never understood how I felt. He didn't know what I was going through. I wanted to die as well; I was totally fucked for months after, and still Pauli went on nagging me about it.

GEORGE
It wasn't your fault. It was just something that happened.

JOHN
I know that, but Pauli didn't see it that way. He wouldn't let go; it was always there somewhere, loitering in the shadows.

GEORGE
Like the proverbial Elephant?

JOHN
Sounds confused by the reference
Elephant?

GEORGE
You know… The "Elephant" in the room…

JOHN
Oh… I see, Elephant, yes…
Pause longer than is necessary.
I suppose so.

GEORGE
Resumes fiddling with the socket.
I thought he would have just let it be, for the sake of the band. We were really good by then; we could have made it…

JOHN

Made it?

Pause

No… not really. The rot had already begun to set in by then. We were already buggered… metaphorically speaking, that is.

GEORGE

Buggered?

George sounds a little confused

JOHN

I think so.

GEORGE

Oh.

JOHN

I did think about you over the years, wondering what happened in your life.

GEORGE

A little surprised

Oh.

George stops fiddling with the socket and sits on the floor again.

JOHN

John flashes George a nonchalant expression.

GEORGE

I thought we were good mates back then?

JOHN

John laughs

We were, but sadly you'd never let me fuck you.

GEORGE

George smiles glibly.

My arse was a temple, and it has always meant something very sacrosanct to me. I wasn't about to let some manwhore fuck it for free.

George smirks at John

JOHN

John laughs

So, you might have considered it if I wasn't shagging everybody else.

GEORGE

You'll never know now, will you?

(Beat)

What about Pete?

JOHN

Nope, I never shagged him either, but I fucked Paul a couple of times when he was pissed and fucked Stuart quite a lot, which is probably why I missed him… I still do from time to time.

GEORGE

A little surprised by John's confession.

No, what I meant was, do you ever see him?

JOHN

Pete? No. Not after we moved down here. I saw him once about fifteen years ago when I went back to Liverpool for a wedding, but not since.

John pours himself another drink.

GEORGE

Whimsically reminiscing.

I lost my cherry in Hamburg, you know… I was only seventeen.

JOHN

John grimaces

To a prozzie, I hope.

GEORGE

I can't remember; all I do know is that it definitely wasn't you.

John laughs.

JOHN

I lost my arse quite a few times in Hamburg as it happens and shagged a lot of whores. I was a right bastard back then. Especially as I'd left Cyn pregnant back in the 'Pool. But she forgave me…

GEORGE

Did she..?

JOHN

He muses

I think so.

GEORGE

So, what happened to you after the band split up?

JOHN

Well, after that wanker at Decca buggered everything up with the recording contract we never got to sign, and we split up - I left Cynthia again and went back to Hamburg for a couple of years and stayed with Astrid. Did some painting, wrote a few books.

GEORGE

Surprised.

Stuart's girlfriend?

JOHN

Yep.

GEORGE

You surprise me, wasn't that a little strange, like being with her?

JOHN

arrogantly

Why? Stuart was dead; she needed a man.

GEORGE

Surprised

And you were it?

JOHN

Yep.

GEORGE

I thought she might have harboured some sort of grudge, at least.

JOHN

No, nothing. Never mentioned it, not once.

GEORGE

She was besotted with Stuart.

JOHN

So was I, in a way, maybe that's how we got through it... together. Stuart was gone, so... we consoled each other. But she left me in the end. She changed... it was never really going to work out.

(Beat)

So, what happened to you?

GEORGE

Went back on the tools. Finished my sparky's apprenticeship, went to work on building sites for nearly forty years. When I was almost sixty, I thought, bugger this. It was getting too cold for me in the winters; the damp was getting into my bones - so I looked around for a nice cushy number inside and started working for this crowd nearly five years ago.

JOHN

Sounds like a pretty boring life to me and nearly all used up now.

GEORGE

It wasn't so bad. Hopefully, I've still got a few more years yet.

JOHN

You never know.

GEORGE

No, I don't suppose we really do. But I'm still happily married after forty years, and we have a son, so I can't complain really. I had to make a living somehow.

I still play a few gigs in pubs at the weekends, just to keep my hand in. But nothing else ever happened after we split, well obviously not - otherwise, you'd be grovelling around on my carpet. I'd be the one having a five o'clock joint and a glass of Jack. You seemed to have done alright?

JOHN

John flashes an expression of resigned acceptance.

Not me really, this is all down to Cyn. I came back from Hamburg after the Astrid thing fizzled out, and Cyn took me back again……

Fuck knows why? I'd been a right bastard and left her to bring Julian up on her own for two years, then deserted her for another two years, but do you know what she said when I knocked on her door.

George shakes his head.

JOHN

"Hello John, are you coming to stay this time?" and I said, "yes, this time I am. And I did."

She said she still loved me; despite everything I had done.

I couldn't understand that – I wanted her to hate me, but she didn't. I wanted her to despise me – but she wouldn't. She just stepped aside and beckoned me in. I asked her why she wasn't screaming at me, and all she said was, she still loved me for all my weaknesses, for all the crap things I'd done to her, she had always known what I was like, and she accepted it.

To me, that defined virtue for its own sake. That was real forgiveness... she'd sacrificed her integrity and her reason. Then she said, to love me for who I once was would have been meaningless - that person had gone. But now, she loved me for what she knew I would become, and that was something else. It was a testament to love and trust and belief, and for that, I could never betray her again, and I never did.....

Pause...

While I had been away, she started writing children's books and then in the early seventies, she became pretty popular.

CONT...

JOHN CONT...

She asked me to do some illustrations for her books, and a little surprisingly, it worked out quite well, all because she believed in me. Sergeant Pepper and his Mysterious Friends, you must have read one of those children's books to your son; they sold a few million copies. We didn't make a fortune, the publishers made all the money, but we made enough to live comfortably for the last forty-odd years. We were very happy, then she went and died. Two years ago...

beat

Two years today, actually.

GEORGE

Oh, Christ, look, I'm sorry, I didn't realise I was intruding, if you want to be alone today, I can come back tomorrow?

JOHN

John holds up his hand.

No need, mate, that's really not necessary. Today I'd rather be with someone I know - someone who also knew her, as it turns out. And anyway, the sky's not working.

beat

Bit weird that... "The Sky's not working" sounds like a bad trip.

John laughs and waves his hands around hippy style.
beat

It's a bit odd, though.. that it chose today to pack up.

47

GEORGE

Why?

JOHN

Because/

GEORGE

George remembers it's the anniversary of Cynthia's death.
/Oh, I see.

beat

I liked Cynthia a lot. We used to have a right laugh when we all went out on the lash.

JOHN

Yea, she was a good sort...

Pause...

We... I... we have a son, Julian, and a daughter Lucy, that's who must have rung you, unbelievably Julian works in a recording studio.

GEORGE

Not at Decca, I hope.

JOHN

No EMI.... Do you know what happened to Pete?

GEORGE

I saw him once in the early ninety's.   The last thing I heard just before I left the 'Pool, he'd started working in the dole office.

John laughs

JOHN

Very Rock and Roll.

GEORGE

It's a living.

JOHN

I liked Pete... fucking useless drummer, but I liked him... I miss him.....

We had a good laugh. Must look Pete up some time; you never know how much time any of us have left these days... or what's around the corner.

Long pause...

I've got cancer, you know; did I mention that?

GEORGE

A little surprised at the revelation

No, you didn't.

JOHN

Bowel and prostate, both outlets buggered. Can't crap or piss...

GEORGE

No shit, that's a bummer.

JOHN

Laughs

"That's very funny, George.

GEORGE

Funny? Oh.

The penny drops

JOHN

It's not too bad. I have to carry this bag around for a year.

He points at his left side, making a wincing expression.
Then I should be okay.

He points to his sparse spikey hair.
I have to have Chemo every month... and get nuked from time to time, but it's no more than I deserve, I suppose.

John smiles at his self-effacing comment.

GEORGE

Probably down to all that extracurricular arse activity in Hamburg

JOHN

Laughs gracefully.

GEORGE

With some trepidation, he asks
Is it tricky...? You know, having a bag, you hear so much about them and...

JOHN

No, not really. Everything is being sorted out slowly. The real problem was everything seemed to happen at the same time. Cynthia died... then I got cancer... and now the bloody broadbands buggered....

JOHN CONT...

John laughs.
George grins but reservedly.
Pause...

I had a heart attack back in 1980; it nearly killed me. I thought I'd been bloody shot...
I got over it, but ever since that day, I have always believed I'd outlived my natural time in this world. So every morning I wake up is a bonus. The fact that I'm still here today is a bloody miracle.

GEORGE

You've been fortunate.

JOHN

I suppose I have.

beat

Cynthia says...

beat

said... every day after that day is a bonus, extra time, time to do something worthwhile. She said it's the most precious commodity we have and we mustn't waste it, and I like to think I didn't.

long beat

It can be fucking hilarious when I fart, you know.

GEORGE

What?

JOHN

When I fart, it's hysterical.

GEORGE

Fart why?

JOHN

The bag fills up quite quickly instead of the gas coming out of my arse.
John gestures a giant balloon inflating by his side.

GEORGE

George smiles but tries to stop himself as he is a little unsure how he should react.

I am sorry, but that does sound bloody hilarious.

JOHN

Don't apologise. It is.

GEORGE

Then what happens?

JOHN

Nothing. It just slowly deflates, so no big explosions, just a little stink.....
What I really miss is you don't get that pleasing sensation of the fart reverberation on the cheeks of your arse - I always enjoyed that part of it. I can't set light to it anymore; that could be a right bloody shit storm. All in all, it's a bit of an anti-climax for what was once a good laugh.

George smiles.

GEORGE
And Paul, what happened to Paul?

JOHN
He played for a while, did a bit of work as a session musician, then wrote a few songs for Cilla and a few others, and they did pretty well. I think he still works in a studio somewhere. He moved down here as well, but I haven't seen him for a while. We have a drink every couple of years and talk about the old days. Two old farts in a pub talking about what might have been. Nobody gives a toss, but then why should they. But he still doesn't forgive me. He pretends he has, but he hasn't.

GEORGE
So at least he made it.

JOHN
Well, sort of, he was never going to give up. He was a musician through and through…
John starts rolling another joint.
But then the world is full of great musicians who might have been famous but for one thing or another… mainly the lack of luck or natural talent, and we didn't have much of either.

GEORGE
I think you're wrong.

JOHN

Wrong? Why?

GEORGE

We could have made some great music together, you know, we were good.

JOHN

You think so?

GEORGE

You and Paul wrote some pretty good songs. We could have been famous, even made some money out of it.

JOHN

Wistfully

We could have been the greatest band the world had ever seen if...

GEORGE

I wouldn't have gone that far. We weren't as good as Cliff and the Shadows.

JOHN

John appears seriously alarmed at this statement.
Oh, for fuck sake, we shit all over Cliff.

GEORGE

That was only my opinion.
A little timidly.

JOHN
John is still a little brusque and changes his attitude.
Well, at least make it an informed one. We could have changed everything with the ideas we had back then. If we'd gone to Eppy and Parlophone records instead of Decca, we could have changed the course of music for the next hundred years. I remember something I read a few years ago by George Carlin; he said…
John pauses to recall the quote.
Some people see things as they are and ask why… but I… I could see how things could have been, and my question was always the same… why not.

GEORGE
Do you really believe that?

JOHN
I do… I did. But it's too late now. We had our chance, and we fucked it up, or should I say that prick at Decca fucked it up by changing his mind. I can't even remember his name.
John takes another toke on the new joint he has rolled and offers it to George once again. George takes it this time.

GEORGE
Nice shit, it's been a long time.
George blows some smoke in the air - revisiting the past.

JOHN
Keep it; I'll roll another one.

GEORGE

Thanks. So, Pauls doing alright?

JOHN

I think he manages to make a decent living. Still writes the odd song, I believe.

GEORGE

Didn't you two ever think about getting back together... you and Paul started out together even before I joined?

JOHN

Yea, we talked about it a few times, we even tried to ring you a couple of times, I'm sure we did, or maybe I just thought about it,

John gazes up at the ceiling as if searching for a long-forgotten memory.

But I couldn't work with Pete - and Ringo, who was going to make the album with us - do you remember Ringo?

GEORGE

Vaguely.

JOHN

Well, he was a bloody good drummer, but he was still playing with Rory Storm, and he didn't want to leave, so it didn't happen. Last I heard, he'd got a residency at Butlins, probably still there now.

GEORGE
Dick, Dick Rowe that was his name, the guy that was going to sign us at Decca.

JOHN
That's right, I remember now. Dick by name … dick by nature and dick by sexual proclivity. He wanted to fuck me as well.

GEORGE
You were extremely popular.

JOHN
With the blokes, I know - but I preferred women. I don't know what it was that set them off. I had to play along to find out what it was all about. I was never sure which way I was leaning, sort of open-minded, non-gender specific LGBTQ+ to use the current vernacular.

GEORGE
It was probably the tight leather trousers we used to wear that did it. They used to crush my nuts.

JOHN
Well, I definitely wouldn't look so good in them these days.

GEORGE
So, you were gay back then?

JOHN

Me! Gay! Fuck no. I just liked a bit of variety, and Stuart gave great head... better than the Kraut prozzies. One of those bitches nearly bit my cock off.

George has another Toke on his joint.

GEORGE

Dick nearly got us a recording contract. It would have been better than nothing.

JOHN

We should have got Epstein, everybody he handled made it big.

GEORGE

George giggles

As I remember, he wanted to handle you personally; that would have made you big...

George giggles again.

JOHN

John laughs aloud.

Very funny, George, but that was just a nasty rumour.

GEORGE

But you were the one spreading the rumour.

JOHN

Oh - was I? I don't remember.

GEORGE

Was he an arse bandit as well?

JOHN

Yes, I think so, everybody seemed to be in those days, and you had to join in if you wanted to get anywhere.

GEORGE

Well, I'm not so sure I would have liked my arse being ravaged by a roundhead, but you could have. It would have been worth it.

JOHN

With an expression of mild derision

You'd pimp me out to a pervy Jew boy just to get a record contract.

GEORGE

If necessary, take one for the band and all that, hey?

JOHN

What about integrity?

GEORGE

Laughing

Fuck integrity if it gets in the way of becoming rich and famous.

JOHN

I thought you said something about fame being an endemic problem that haunts the proletariat masses; I was just beginning to warm to you.

GEORGE

Naa, just making conversation.

JOHN

You soon changed your mind then?

GEORGE

Needs must when the devil whips your arse.

JOHN

Oh. True loyalty, then?

GEORGE

You would have loved to batter him around a bit. That was your thing...

JOHN

Looks stunned.

GEORGE

Sorry, that was a cheap shot.

JOHN

John smiles.

Yea, well, it's a bit too late now. But would it really have made any difference in the end? All Eppy's bum buddy bands made it big but never made any money, and where are they now? Still on the road scratching out a living in working men's clubs without a pot to piss in.

beat

At least we held on to our integrity.

GEORGE

Yea, but the money would have been good. We could have been millionaires. We could have bought new cars and nice houses. I always fancied an enormous gothic mansion with a big garden. Loved gardening, but I live in a flat now, so I have to settle for a couple of pot plants. Rich and famous would have been good. I could have done that.

JOHN

Reflectively

I always wanted to buy a big Rolls Royce and paint it with brightly coloured flowers and drive around London, just to stick it up the establishment.

beat

Do you really think we could have made it?

GEORGE

Yes, we were a good band. You and Paul wrote some good songs; you could have written a few more, think of all those royalties.   We could have made a good album, maybe two.

JOHN

You really think so? I didn't see the point.

GEORGE

As you said, we could have been the biggest band in the world. We could have made a difference.

JOHN

Na, I don't think so, not really. It was just a pipe dream, a bubble, and it would have burst eventually. It always does... it did.

GEORGE

You pricked the bubble.

JOHN

Did I?

GEORGE

Could have been nicer to Eppy. Maybe he would have signed us instead of Dick. You and Paul wrote your own songs; nobody else did. I even managed to write a few.

JOHN

George, I don't wish to be offensive, especially as we have only just met again after fifty-odd years, but, and I say this in the nicest possible way, our songs were pretty good; your songs were mainly shit. I remember that much, that instrumental we wrote together was a fucking musical travesty.

GEORGE

But they were getting better.

JOHN

Were they?

GEORGE

I had some beautiful ideas for some songs we could have used.

JOHN

Naa, they were mainly shit, George.   Take it from me; they were rubbish. Stick to mending Sky boxes. That's regular work.

GEORGE

Slightly offended by John's short put down.
Well, we'll never know now, will we, but I think you're wrong.

JOHN

Maybe, it has been known… occasionally.

It goes quiet for about half a minute. George fiddles with a cable socket, and John wanders around the room.

GEORGE

Do you remember that Shea Stadium thing that Mick and the Stones did in 65? That was good.

JOHN

Couldn't hear a bloody word, but my telly was crap, so that didn't help. I ran into one of their roadies in the pub just after they came back from that tour, and do you know what he told me he remembered most?

GEORGE

Drinking, screaming and sex, probably?

JOHN

No, stinking piss.

GEORGE

Piss?

JOHN

Apparently, if a girl managed to get to the front of the stage and then realised she needed a pee, she would just do it right there, rather than lose her place, so you can imagine how bad it must have stunk after a couple of hours,... like a Benghazi Khazi.

They both laugh.

GEORGE

Whenever I see it, I always think that it could have been us. We were that good - better even.

John moves over to a small bar in the corner, pours out two Jack Daniels, brings them over to where George is sitting and offers him one of the glasses.

JOHN

Definitely the smelliest...
George smiles
I'll tell you what I think, George...

GEORGE

What?

JOHN

You've just become an old dreamer lost in the hazy, crazy passage of time.

GEORGE

Weren't we all dreamers back then?
pause
Don't we all start out as romantic visionaries...
Surely that's how it is with every musician...?

JOHN

Maybe, but then we become realists and pragmatic, or else we'd starve to death.

GEORGE

Is that really you speaking, or has someone stolen the real John Lennon I used to know?

John smiles

JOHN

You were a half-decent guitarist George, I'll give you that, but we were never that good as a band. Anyway, America would have killed us stone dead, didn't do Cliff any good and look what happened to Mick. Some crazy nutter shoots him in the back in the middle of New York, for Christ sake, just because he felt like it. So, Mick became very rich, but unfortunately, he's also been very dead for the last forty years.   I'm perfectly content in Croydon, collecting my pension and living my life in quiet obscurity.

GEORGE

I always looked up to you John, I thought you were a god... did you know that?

JOHN

What, like Stuart?

GEORGE

No, you were different. There was something, I don't know what, but I would have followed you to...

JOHN

Please don't tell me you're an arse bandit as well. I can't bum fuck you with this colostomy bag - it would be another bloody shit storm.

GEORGE

No, I'm not gay; I was just saying I admired how you could hold a crowd back in the Cavern days. You always had them in the palm of your hand. We could have built something on that. Together just for that one fleeting moment in time, we were magic.

JOHN

John smiles appreciatively
Tell you what, George, sing me one of your songs?

GEORGE

What?

JOHN

One of your songs, sing me one.

GEORGE

You'll only say it's shit and take the piss and…

JOHN

Laughing
/Oh, excellent George, very amusing. Relentlessly mocking the afflicted.

GEORGE

Sorry I didn't mean it like that. I…

JOHN

No, it's alright. I probably deserve it anyway.
Go on, sing me one of your bloody songs. I
need a laugh.

GEORGE

I haven't got my guitar with me.

JOHN

John shakes his finger at George
Luckily, I have.

*John passes a guitar to George, who stands up and sits on
the arm of a sofa*
*Lights go down, and the first few bars of "While my Guitar
gently Weeps" play in darkness.*

I look at you all, see the love there that's
sleeping,
While my guitar gently weeps…

The song fades out after a couple of minutes seconds
The lights come up, and John claps gently.

JOHN

Better than expected.
Beat

But we wouldn't have got rich or famous with
that. It's a bit dreary and pedestrian, and there's
no message. It would have been forgotten in a
few months…
Beat
Hesitantly
but I did like it.

68

GEORGE

And Twist and Shout had a message?

JOHN

I didn't write that piece of crap. It just worked on stage. We would have to have written all our own songs to have got anywhere. We couldn't have done that. We weren't that good. You have to be Jewish to write a perfect song, and I'm not chopping the end of my nob off just so I can write a decent song.

GEORGE

Stunned

What?

JOHN

Jewish, you have to be Jewish to write really good songs. It's what they do.

GEORGE

Who fed you that horseshit?

JOHN

Nobody. It's a fact. George Gershwin, Irving Berlin, Lionel Bart, Andrew Lloyd Webber, they're proper writers.

GEORGE

Lloyd Webber isn't Jewish.

JOHN

Are you sure?

GEORGE

Yes.

JOHN

Well, most of it was shite anyway, so you're probably right on that one.

GEORGE

He's worth half a billion quid, you know?

JOHN

Is he?

GEORGE

So, he can't be that bad.

JOHN

There's no accounting for taste - anyway... money isn't everything.

GEORGE

It is when you haven't got any.

JOHN

John smiles and ponders for a few moments.
I'll tell you what. I'll sing you one of my songs then you can tell me what you think about it?

They are both now showing signs of being a little stoned

GEORGE

Yea, go on then.

John wanders over to sit at the piano and plays around with a few chords for a moment or two...
Lights go down

JOHN SINGS "IMAGINE"

.

Songs ends
Lights come up

GEORGE

Well, it's not exactly rock and roll, a bit ploddy actually, not very cheerful...

He bobs his head from side to side slowly with a mournful expression and hums a small part of the song as a dirge.

JOHN

John is a little outraged by George's comment and replies disdainfully

We would have moved on to other more adventurous things eventually.

GEORGE

Expectantly
Jollier?

JOHN

Jollier! I don't write jolly fucking songs

John appears distraught at the suggestion and pretends to choke. George seems a little surprised at John's reaction.

GEORGE

In the spirit of compromise.
Up-tempo, then?

JOHN

Possibly. We did have a hard edge once when we were a rock and roll band.

GEORGE

Yes, we did. That's why I look back on those days with pride.

JOHN

Looking back is a waste of time George, we're all going in the other direction.

GEORGE

I suppose we all mellow as we get older, so we start writing nostalgic songs about how things might have been.

JOHN

In the moment?

GEORGE

Exactly.

JOHN

We were "fab" back then
John high double digits the word "fab."

GEORGE

Yes, so the band might have worked out?

JOHN

John takes another toke on his joint

Maybe, maybe not. Anything was possible in those days, absolutely anything. They managed to put a man on the moon, for Christ's sake, so us making a half-decent record was hardly pushing the boundaries of artistic endeavour.

GEORGE

beat

Do you really think we could have been bigger than Cliff?

JOHN

John is stunned.

Fuck! We could have been more popular than Jesus.

GEORGE

George appears stunned by that assertion

So, bigger than Cliff and Jesus?

JOHN

No, I didn't mean it like that. I just think that people are less reliant on religion these days. They don't need it like they used to - they don't trust the church anymore, not like before. I mean, it's just a business like any other, making money from renting property - investing a bit in the stock market and arranging singsongs on Sunday... and Christmas. And we have got internet now... when it works.

He points at the television derisorily

GEORGE

But people still go to church, so they must get something from it, and it doesn't cost them anything?

JOHN

Not while they're alive, no. Their biggest money earner is from people close to death. These people desperately desire salvation while grasping hopelessly for the meaning of life and a free pass to heaven. That's their biggest seller, a ticket to ride to the other side. Everybody needs to believe in something near the end; otherwise, what's the point. That's where the church comes in, but not Jesus.

GEORGE

So, what do you believe in?

JOHN

Good question, what do I believe in?   ......
Nothing. I don't believe in anything except maybe music.

GEORGE

I don't understand.

JOHN

Well, as I just said, I don't believe in religion;
that's just an enormous illusion created a few
thousand years ago by some crafty buggers who
thought they could blag the rest of the world
into being good by frightening us into believing
that if we were naughty, we would go to hell...
but there is no hell, and there definitely isn't
any heaven. So, all that praying lark is just a
waste of time and effort... It's all about power
and control of the proletariat masses, or it was.

I don't believe what the newspapers say
because they only print what the politicians
want us to know, so how do we know if it's
really the truth? And television's no different.
We are force-fed what they want us to believe.
Everything is censored or redacted. There is so
little truth these days that when you hear it,
which is very rare, you don't see it for what it is
because it's lost in all the lies and fake news, so
how can we really know one from the other?

GEORGE

Maybe it was best we did break up when we
did. I hate to think what could have happened to
the world if you'd gone from being a bitter
musician rebelling against the establishment to
a nihilistic delusional cynic on a mission to
destroy all the political, social and religious
institutions.

JOHN

What, you would have been afraid of hearing me tell the truth?

GEORGE

But is the world ready for the truth? Is any of us prepared for that? Can you imagine…

JOHN

Imagine!
George smiles at that word.

GEORGE

Yes, but can you imagine a world without a single lie? We would hurt people every day by speaking the truth instead of saying nothing and keeping it to ourselves.

JOHN

But isn't that the problem?.. people not speaking out. Under this cover of deceit, terrible things happen, where they flourish and become something much worse.

GEORGE

I don't see how?

JOHN

Fanatical terrorists! What do they want?

GEORGE

I don't know. Does anybody really know what they want?

JOHN

Well, they must want something, but no one ever bothers to ask them. Maybe if someone spoke to them, they would stop killing people. The talking stopped the problems in Ireland.

GEORGE

I think you're oversimplifying the situation; it really isn't as easy as that. Terrorists of today want something completely different from what they wanted in Ireland.

JOHN

Then we should try to find out what it is.

GEORGE

Maybe they want something that isn't available anymore?

JOHN

Like what?

GEORGE

I don't know, but maybe that's what everybody is looking for, something new that doesn't exist yet but perhaps may suddenly materialise in a puff of smoke one day.

JOHN

What like a Jehovah's Witness?

GEORGE

George smiles

They do exist. I just don't know where they come from. They're like Big Issue sellers... suddenly appearing like a genie out of a bottle.

JOHN

Maybe it's all McDonald's fault?

GEORGE

McDonald's?

JOHN

The world has gone very crazy in the last fifty years, and coincidently that's how long McDonalds has been around. I blame them. They put something in the burgers.

GEORGE

So, now you're blaming McDonald's for all the madness in the world?

JOHN

Possibly.

GEORGE

You think there's a drug in the burgers that turns people into psychopaths and fanatical religious terrorist's?

JOHN

Absolutely. I've always found those pickled gherkins to be very suspect.

GEORGE

George glances at John with a strangely quizzical expression

But McDonald's customers can't all turn into religious nutters after eating just one burger. That doesn't make any sense. The world would be overrun with terrorists by lunchtime.

JOHN

Contemplatively

Maybe there's a subversive chemical element in gherkins that has a progressively detrimental effect - building up over the years and eventually affecting people's brains.

GEORGE

With a distinct hint of improbability.

Hitler or Saddam Hussein didn't eat McDonald's. In fact, Hitler was a vegetarian.

JOHN

Ah, but we don't know that for sure. That's only what we've been told by the newspapers.

John flashes an expression of didactic disbelief at George and waggles his index finger contemptuously.

GEORGE

Anyway, McDonald's weren't even around in the nineteen forties.

JOHN

Maybe not, but they did have those delicious Bratwurst sausages with mustard. They could be very seditious, especially if you put Sauerkraut on top.

GEORGE

Don't you mean delicious?

JOHN

John glares at George disbelievingly.
No…

GEORGE

Indicating disbelief at John's ramblings.
So, what you're saying is burgers and bangers turn harmless grazers into pathological psycho killers and sociopaths?

John doesn't reply but just makes a vague wincing expression.

George fiddles around with the Sky-box.

GEORGE

beat
I can't find anything wrong with the signal on this box. Where's your broadband router?

JOHN

Over there.

John points to the television.

George sits down on the floor next to the router/cable socket.

Long pause.

GEORGE

So, I presume it must have been your daughter Lucy who phoned us about the problem.

JOHN

Yes, it was.

GEORGE

How old is she now?

JOHN

Lucy is Forty-one, and Julian is nearly forty-eight. We were very young when he was born.

GEORGE

And you see them quite a bit, I guess?

JOHN

More so since Cynthia died. In fact, Lucy pops in most nights now since she split up from her partner.

GEORGE

Well, that's good. I mean, it's good she pops in, not so good that she's split up.

JOHN

No, it wasn't good for her, but for me... well, I do miss someone to talk to, and her partner was a pratt.

Pause

GEORGE

George is fiddling with the cables.
Beat
Beat

I wonder what would have happened had we made an album, but with Brian as our manager.

JOHN

Laughs

We'd probably be superstars.

GEORGE

But would we still be here?

JOHN

What do you mean?

GEORGE

Well, look at Jagger – biggest band in the world for years then shot dead at thirty. Keith, dead after a nasty accident with his lawnmower, and Brian drowned in his swimming pool, maybe that's the price you pay for fame.

JOHN

No, I don't think so. Those things would have happened no matter what.

GEORGE

Jagger moved to New York to get away from the fans, but would he have been shot in Hackney - if no one knew him.... Would Brian have drowned if he didn't have a pool? And Keith, well, would he have bought a monster sit on mower if he didn't have a garden?

JOHN

You could go on all day with theories like that, Elvis, Keith Moon, Jim Morrison...
Burgers were definitely to blame for Elvis's death.

George smiles

GEORGE

My question is, would it have made any difference. Maybe if we had made the big time, we wouldn't be having this conversation right now on account of us both being dead?

JOHN

You're a little bit scary at times, do you know that? not the quiet little George Hamilton/

GEORGE

/Harrison!

JOHN

Surprised.
Harrison?

GEORGE

Yes

JOHN

Are you sure? I thought your name was…

GEORGE

Of course I'm bloody sure.

JOHN

John smiles
/Sorry, not the George Harrison I used to know.
He was very quiet and unassuming.

GEORGE

I've changed a bit over the years.

JOHN

So I see.

GEORGE

It's Karma, mate.

JOHN

Karma?

GEORGE
The road of destiny down which we all must travel. It defines who we are and what will happen to us. All the things we must do - we have done, all the things we have to do - will be done.

George adopts a transcendental lotus position on the floor, holding his arms out - palms facing upwards and begins waving them around as if in a psychotropic trance.

JOHN
John pretends not to take any notice of George.
Does it?

GEORGE
George resumes working on the router.
I know some people just die no matter what, but sometimes I believe something happens that allows other forces to control our lives when we search for fame. Maybe we leave a tiny door open to our soul and let the devil in?

JOHN
John thinks about that for a few moments
Well, whatever it is, it didn't get us.

GEORGE
No, it didn't. And for that, we must give thanks to the gods.

JOHN
John sardonically
And it didn't get Cliff either.

GEORGE
No, Cliff has God on his side. He beat the odds.

JOHN
I thought you had to have the devil on your side
to beat the odds?

GEORGE
No, I don't believe that either…

Long pause…

George points at a strange wooden object similar to a chair in the centre of the room. It has no parallel or perpendicular planes and a pointed vertical shaft in the middle.
Tell me something… What is that it has been
puzzling me, ever since I arrived?

JOHN
It's Norwegian, Norwegian wood actually, they
are famous for their wood.

GEORGE
I thought it was meatballs.

JOHN
Looking confused.
Meatballs?

GEORGE
That's what Norwegians are famous for.

JOHN

No, that's Ikea.

GEORGE

Ikea? Oh.

JOHN

This is a piece of Modern art from Norway.
John walks around the object admiring it.
I bought it last week. Ikea is Swedish, by the way, not Norwegian. They are the meatball people.

George acknowledges Johns correction and continues to gaze at the object with some concern.

GEORGE

Modern art?

JOHN

Yes. It's an existential affectation of life, the artist's interpretation of the nihilistic world encapsulated in a single object... a chair. The horizontal angles represent the integration of all races and cultures, and the vertical planes represent conflicting political opinions.   It's called "The Thinking Chair."

GEORGE

George points at the horizontal spike coming up through the centre of the piece.
And the sharp pointy bit.

JOHN

Said with didactic pretension
Ahh, that's religion… all religions, in fact.

GEORGE

Looks very uncomfortable for a chair, more like a pile of driftwood, some desperate castaway nailed together in a blind panic to escape from somewhere, anywhere in fact…

JOHN

It's not supposed to be a chair you can sit on; it's a metaphor.

GEORGE

A Metaphor?

JOHN

Yes.

GEORGE

Not a chair you sit on?

JOHN

No.

GEORGE

Then is it really a chair? If you can't sit on it?

JOHN

Yes, George,

John sounds exasperated.

You have to understand the more profound philosophical message of art... the true meaning... it is a chair... a chair to sit on and think, and... meditate, but you sit on it transcendentally, not physically, that's the idea.

GEORGE

I still can't see the point.

George is touching the top of the shaft protruding from the chair vertically. He is not taking it too seriously, and this is visibly frustrating John.

JOHN

Tersely

You are not supposed to touch it. That will disturb the cosmic vibrations flowing from within.

GEORGE

George looks on with contained amusement.

Cosmic vibes?

JOHN

Yes.

GEORGE

Beat

A bit like Karma, then?

JOHN

I suppose so… a bit.

GEORGE

I never really understood the purpose of philosophy. I always presumed it was the intellectual's way of explaining the meaning of life to plebs.

JOHN

No, it's the other way around, actually.

GEORGE

Appearing confused
I don't understand.

JOHN

Philosophy is there specifically to prove there is no meaning to life.

GEORGE

Hmm, I see, or maybe not… and those?
George points at the two Ikea chairs.

JOHN

They are Ikea, the meatball people, Sweden. I don't like them very much, never did, to be honest, but Cynthia loved them, so they stayed, but I'll probably get rid of them, now she's gone.

GEORGE

I like them.

JOHN

Well, take them when you go. A present from Cynthia and me for all the fun we had all those years ago.

GEORGE

Are you sure?

JOHN

Of course I am. They're only inanimate objects in a material world.

GEORGE

But you said they were important to you, part of a memory.

JOHN

Precisely, and that's my point. You must challenge the manacle of materialism from time to time and try to break the chain.

GEORGE

How?

JOHN

Take something precious and important to you, something that you can't live without... and give it away... then you will break the yoke of possession that is weighing you down.

GEORGE
Are they that important to you?
George says this tongue in cheek.

JOHN
Yes, I suppose so. I could give you my stoma
bag if you prefer, that is also very precious to
me.

GEORGE
I'll stick with the chairs if it's all the same.
They're fine, thanks…
Beat
What about the telly?

JOHN
Fuck off.

*George picks up the banjo, starts playing different riffs, and
then begins strumming the chords to All Those Years Ago.
Played with a singalong banjo rhythm.*

I'm   shouting   all   about   love
While   they   treated   you   like   a   dog
When you were the one who had made it so
clear
All those years ago. The lights go down as the
song fades away after the second verse.
Lights come back up.
*John doesn't say anything for a few moments but just stares
at George*

JOHN

George… I must apologise.

GEORGE

Why have you farted?

JOHN

John laughs.

No, no, I haven't, but I have just heard one of the best songs I never wrote.

GEORGE

You liked it.

JOHN

I liked it. It's everything it should be, and I apologise for saying all your songs were shite. That one wasn't.

GEORGE

Not shite?

JOHN

No, definitely not shite.

GEORGE

George is lost for words for a few moments?

Well, thank you, John, that means a lot to me, thank you.

JOHN

John gets up and walks towards the bathroom
> Right, well, I have to empty my bag; all this excitement has made me crap myself.

Lights go down

END OF SCENE

SCENE TWO

Lucy arrives the Same day at 5.00pm

The doorbell rings and John stands up and walks over to open the door. George stays seated. Lucy comes in. They hug.

LUCY
Hello dad, how are you today?
Lucy is carrying a bag of fish and chips, she gives them to John. John puts them on the kitchen worktop.

JOHN
Better for seeing you, oh I didn't know you'd rung the Sky people.

LUCY
You ask me to.

JOHN
Did I?

LUCY
Yes. Have they come yet?

JOHN
Yes, he's here; it's George, the Skyman.

LUCY
Lucy looks puzzled.
George the Sky man, how come you know his name?

JOHN

Well, you're not going to believe this, but many, many years ago we were in a band together playing nightclubs in Germany.

LUCY

Lucy smirks
During the war?

JOHN

No. It wasn't during the fucking war.
John scoffs.

LUCY

Lucy reprimands John
Dad!
It must have been a long time ago.

JOHN

It was. I was just twenty. George was even younger.

GEORGE

Everybody's younger than you, Lennon.
George smiles at Lucy.

JOHN

Say hello to George Lucy, he knew your mum.

LUCY

Hello George, nice to meet you.
George jumps to his feet and puts his hand out. They shake hands a little cautiously at first.
So, you two were in a band together?

GEORGE

For our sins.

JOHN

And there were lots of those...
Lucy flashes John a scornful expression.

JOHN

Would you like a cup of tea Luce?

LUCY

Yea, go on...
She turns to George.
So, you knew my mum?

GEORGE

Yea, I knew Cyn. I was sorry to hear that....

LUCY

Lucy smiles. She is trying to gauge George.

GEORGE

We all grew up together, you know. I'm sorry I missed her funeral, we sort of lost touch over the years.

Lucy smiles.

LUCY
People do, unfortunately.
Lucy turns to John.
There's not enough for three, I'm sorry.
John moves to the kitchenette area and starts unpacking the fish and chips onto two plates

GEORGE
Hey, don't worry about me. I'll be finished soon,   then I'll be off. I'll leave you two in peace.

LUCY
I don't think dad knew where you lived; otherwise, I'm sure he would have contacted you about mum.

GEORGE
I'm sure he would, but he wouldn't have known. We haven't seen each other since the sixties. It's such a pity we all lose track of friends over time. I would have liked to have said goodbye.
It goes quiet for a few seconds.
I bet John never told you I could have wound up being your father?

LUCY
Looking surprised?
How? were you having an affair with mum? I heard it was all very liberated in the sixties, but that's…

GEORGE

No, nothing like that. We were in the registry office, just the three of us. The service had just started when some workers started using jackhammers outside at the back of the building. It was absolutely deafening. The whole building was reverberating, and we couldn't hear a damn thing.

John starts smiling

Anyway, the registrar asked the groom to step forward, and I thought I heard him say the best man, so I stepped up. It was only when we were halfway through the service that John stuck his nose in and said he was supposed to be marrying Cynthia, not me. Bloody hilarious. We pissed ourselves for ages over that. Your dad said something about nearly having a lucky escape… but Cynthia didn't find it very was amusing.

LUCY

Sounds just like dad.

GEORGE

There are other things I could tell you, but I won't. The old fellah would kill me.

LUCY

Look, I have to be somewhere tonight, so would you rather stay and have dinner with dad, and I'll pop off. I'm sure you two have lots to catch up on. I can come back later.

GEORGE

I don't know about that, from what John has been saying, he looks forward to having his dinner with you on Friday night.

LUCY

I'm sure it will be alright… he needs to talk to old friends whenever possible, it helps.

GEORGE

Helps?

LUCY

He's become a little "forgetful" since mum died; she did everything for him.

GEORGE

Oh, I see.

JOHN

John mumbles
I haven't gone deaf yet.

LUCY

She turns to John
Dad, I've got to pop out for a while, but I'll come back later before I go home. Do you want to have dinner with George instead of me tonight? There's only enough for two.

JOHN

Are you sure Lucy, it is our night?

LUCY

I know that, but old friends from way back when don't turn up every day. We'll always have next week for dinner.

JOHN

That would be great, thanks, Lucy

Lucy crosses the room and kisses John on the head. Then crosses over to George and gives him a hug and a kiss on the cheek.

LUCY

It was lovely to meet you, my "nearly dad."
George smiles.

GEORGE

It was great to meet you too.

LUCY

Turning to John
By the way… What is that?
She points at the Thinking Chair, smiling.

JOHN

John glances at George then back at Lucy and smiles
I'm glad you like it, it's Norwegian. Norwegian wood, actually, that's what they are famous for.

LUCY

I thought that was meatballs.

JOHN

Looking confused.
> No, it's not bloody meatballs. That's the fucking swedes.

LUCY
> Ooooh, daddy.

Mock castigation
beat
> It's a bloody disaster though, isn't it?

JOHN
> No. It's not. It's Modern art. It originally came from Norway. I bought it last week.

Argumentatively

LUCY
> Did you?

beat
> Modern art?

JOHN

He blurts this out in a repetitive monotonic manner as if he were a tour guide at a museum.
> Yes. The artist's interpretation of a nihilistic world. It's an existential affectation of life, encapsulated in a single object... a chair. The horizontal angles represent all races, cultures and religions intertwined. The vertical planes represent a convergence of conflicting religious opinions, and the central core is tranquillity. It's called "The Thinking Chair."

LUCY

Oh. Is it? Doesn't look much like a chair to me. Not you could sit on and have a quiet think, well not with that pointy thing sticking up your arse...

Cynthia fondles the spiky bit.

Looks more like a pile of old firewood that's been nailed together by a drunken monkey.

JOHN

Oh, for fucks sake, it's not supposed to be a chair you can sit on.

LUCY

confused

Not a chair you sit on?

JOHN

No.

LUCY

Then is it really a chair? If you can't sit on it?

JOHN

Yes, Lucy,

John sounds exasperated.

You have to embrace the more profound philosophical message, the true meaning... it is a chair... a chair you sit on and meditate, but you sit on it transcendentally, not physically. It emanates a serene aura.

George nods fawningly in agreement.

LUCY
I think it would emanate a great deal of pain…
in the arse.
Lucy is still quizzically caressing the top of the shaft.

JOHN
You are not supposed to touch the pointy bit.
That disturbs the cosmic flow of karmic
waves…

LUCY
Karmic waves?
*Lucy looks amused but restrains herself from making any
further comment.*

JOHN
Yes.

GEORGE
Drolly
Is that like a discharge of tranquillity?

JOHN
Looks at George disdainfully
No. It doesn't discharge anything; it radiates…

LUCY
Lucy smiles at her dad.
Right. I'll be off then, see you later, have fun
with your pointy chair…

John smiles.

Lucy leaves, and John and George sit down and start to eat their fish and chips.

GEORGE

She's a great girl.

JOHN

Yes, she is, and Julian's a good kid too. I'm glad I was able to be with them most of their lives.

GEORGE

That's a strange thing to say.

JOHN

Why aren't you glad you were around every day to watch your son grow up.

GEORGE

Well, yes, of course.

JOHN

We could have lost all that, every precious moment missed and lost forever. You can't get that back you know.

GEORGE

Still not with you... These chips are nice.

JOHN

Yea, they do fry excellent chips... and that's what's important.

GEORGE

A little surprised
What? Nice chips?

JOHN

No, seeing your kids grow up... that's what I would have missed; that's what's important. If we'd been famous, we would probably never have seen them or maybe only on the odd weekend.

GEORGE

If we had been, but we weren't, so we did see them grow up, so it worked out best in the end... good Karma?

JOHN

John smiles
Best for who, I wonder?

GEORGE

Best for us and our kids.

JOHN

I still think we could have brought something unique to the world, something that could have lasted forever.

GEORGE

Really?

JOHN

Yes.

GEORGE

Do you really think we would have made any difference?

JOHN

Yes, I did. For a long time, but I'm not so sure now.

GEORGE

But at what price, and would it really have lasted forever? Does anything last forever.

JOHN

We'll never know now, will we?

GEORGE

No, we won't, but I am happy with the way things turned out. Aren't you happy John, it wasn't so bad, was it?

JOHN

Yea, I'm happy, but Christ, I miss Cynthia. Can't believe I will never see her again.

GEORGE

George nods.

So, if you had the chance, would you go back and do it all again and maybe change a few things, so we did become famous?

JOHN

Ponders over George's question for a few moments
No, I wouldn't. I have learned that life is what happens while you're busy making plans or trying to change the world. I've had a good life, seen my children grow up, and I have been there. What more is there, really? Fame… you can keep it.

George gets up from the table and takes his plate over to the sink to wash it, then walks back over to the router box he was working on, checks a meter he has in his hand and starts to replace the socket.

GEORGE

The television comes on.
There you go, broadbands back, everything should be working now.

JOHN

Thank you George.

GEORGE

No, thank you, John, for what might have been and for what is. I think I prefer the what is, though.

JOHN

Me to… me to.

GEORGE

And thanks for dinner.

JOHN

No problem, any time, and don't forget to pop back tomorrow for the chairs.

GEORGE

I will, we can have another chat.

JOHN

And maybe play a few songs.

GEORGE

Yea maybe.

They both walk to the front door, hug and then part. John closes the door, walks back to the sofa, sits down, turns the television off, and stares at the screen.

Lights fade, and we segue to the next scene.

SCENE THREE Cynthia enters.

Dream Sequence.
Same day later 7.00pm

Cynthia is sitting on the Sofa. John is pouring a drink by the piano.

JOHN

John waggles his glass at Cynthia.
Drink Cyn?

CYNTHIA

No, I'm OK, thanks,

beat

So, how are you, how have you been?

JOHN

I'll be better once I get this down.

CYNTHIA

No, I meant how are you, in yourself?

JOHN

Good, I'm good.

CYNTHIA

We should be celebrating or something; It seems strange doing nothing.

JOHN

John appears confused

Doing nothing?

beat

But I am, in a manner of speaking. You're here; that's doing something, isn't it?

CYNTHIA

I suppose so.

JOHN

And celebrating your death, that's a little strange.

CYNTHIA

You think so?

JOHN

Well, it's not normal.

CYNTHIA

We're not normal though, are we, John?

JOHN

Aren't we? No, maybe not.

beat

CYNTHIA

Was there someone here just before I arrived?

JOHN

John turns to Cynthia and smiles.

You don't miss much, do you?

CYNTHIA

I don't have much else to do these days.

JOHN

So, you keep an eye on me?

CYNTHIA

Well, sort of, but not in a weird way. I don't go peeping through keyholes or anything like that. I just watch over you.

JOHN

Hmmm.

Beat

George, it was George who was here earlier.

CYNTHIA

George?

JOHN

Harrison.

CYNTHIA

Christ, that's a blast from the/

JOHN

/Should you be saying that?

CYNTHIA

What? Blast?

JOHN

No… Christ!

CYNTHIA

He doesn't mind.

JOHN

Oh… so he's…?
John waves his hands around in a majestic flourish.

CYNTHIA

Omnipresent

JOHN

Omnipresent?

CYNTHIA

Oh yes. Knows and sees everything.

JOHN

Oh, does he? Well, I'm in trouble with all the pain and grief I've brought you.

CYNTHIA

No, I don't think so; he forgives most things.

JOHN

Oh good.

CYNTHIA

So, how is George, my nearly husband?

JOHN

Yes, he nearly was, wasn't he? Funny you should mention that.

CYNTHIA

Why?

JOHN

Well, it came up in conversation today when Lucy popped in.

Cynthia smiles

CYNTHIA

How is our Lucy?

JOHN

She's good. Split up from her partner, but I never really liked him anyway.

CYNTHIA

There's a lot of people you don't like.

JOHN

He wasn't nice to her; I'm glad it's over. I didn't tell her that, you don't do you?

Cynthia shakes her head.

CYNTHIA

How does Lucy feel about it?

JOHN

Deep down, I think she's relieved, she doesn't say much, but she seems happier.

CYNTHIA

That's good... so what's George been doing all these years?

JOHN

Not much, as it turns out.

CYNTHIA

Did he give up the music world the same as you?

JOHN

Brusquely

I didn't give it up; it threw me out

CYNTHIA

Sorry, did I touch a nerve?

JOHN

No... It was just something else George said. It made me think back to all those years ago.

CYNTHIA

And what?

JOHN

He said we shouldn't have packed it in, should have kept going, might have even made the big time.

CYNTHIA

Did he...? well, maybe you should have.

JOHN

No, I don't think so. I'm happy with the way things turned out except for you, that is.

CYNTHIA

Except for me... was I a mistake then?

John smiles

JOHN

No, you weren't a mistake, but you left me much too early... now I'm alone till I die.

CYNTHIA

I'm sorry about that, but there was nothing I could do about it. Now, maybe you know just a little how it feels to be alone.

JOHN

I know, it's just... it's just so bloody miserable at times talking to myself.

CYNTHIA

I'm here today.

JOHN

But you only come once a year. I've only seen you twice since you died.

CYNTHIA

That's the rules, I'm sorry.

JOHN

Hmmm.

CYNTHIA

I'm sure you could find someone else.

JOHN

I don't think so; it would never be quite the same.

CYNTHIA

Isn't that the point of someone new?

JOHN

John smiles

The front door rings, John gets up to answer it.
Are you going to stay? I think it's just my housekeeper.

CYNTHIA

I will stay as long as you want me to stay tonight.

JOHN

Good…. Good.

Yoni enters - it is early evening.
 She speaks with a slightly dislocated Japanese accent, leaving out the odd indefinite article…
YONI cannot see Cynthia.

YONI

Hello John, how are you today?
Yoni takes off her coat and hangs it up.

JOHN

I'm good, Yoni, how about you?

YONI

I'm okay, thank you. Sorry, I late tonight, busy
day.
*Yoni takes out a housecoat she has been carrying in a
Tesco's bag and puts it on.*

JOHN

No problem, I'm not going anywhere.

YONI

Anything special you want me to do today?

JOHN

Just the usual bathroom and kitchen, you know
and don't forget to get right into the corners.

YONI

No Johnny Boy, I no forget corners.

JOHN

That's where all the bugs hide.

YONI

She Shrugs but says nothing....

YONI

Okay, I not forget corners... Have you had something to eat? I could make sandwich if you like before I start?

JOHN

No, it's okay, Yoni. Lucy popped in earlier with fish and chips.

YONI

Oh good. Only I do worry about you being on your own and not eating properly.

She moves to the kitchen area and takes some cleaning items out of a cupboard.
Cynthia flashes John a curious glance.

JOHN

You shouldn't; I'll survive. I'm a big boy now.

YONI

Yoni smiles

I know that Johnny Boy.

JOHN

I'm not your problem, Yoni, you must have plenty of your own to think about without worrying about me?

YONI

I have a few… but you know Johnny, each one of us must look out for the other, or we are all doomed. That's the covenant of life.

Cynthia flashes John an expression of mocking affection. John flashes Cynthia an expression of caustic censure.

JOHN

That sounds a bit gloomy Yoni, who said that?

YONI

confused

I did, just now.

JOHN

No, sorry, Yoni, what I meant was who originally said it… Plato?

YONI

I don't know. I read it on Salvation Army poster I saw as I was driving here today.

JOHN

Oh, I see.

John smiles.

Yoni wanders off to the bathroom.

CYNTHIA

She seems nice! A little strange, but nice.

A brief expression of approval flashes over Cynthia's face.

JOHN

John flashes Cynthia an expression of rebuke and replies abruptly.

Nice! She's my cleaner.

CYNTHIA

Smiles

I know that, but... she's right, you shouldn't be alone.

JOHN

Well, you shouldn't have left me.

CYNTHIA

I had no choice. Maybe you should think about?...

JOHN

No thanks. If I start screwing Yoni and we fell out, I will have to start doing my own cleaning again, so no... I prefer to hang onto her as a cleaner if you don't mind.

beat

CYNTHIA

So, what happened to Jane? She was our cleaner for years, before...

JOHN

I started screwing her, we fell out, she buggered off, and I was left to do the cleaning!

JOHN

John beams at Cynthia with a resigned expression and holds his hands out, palms upward.

CYNTHIA

Oh, I see. You didn't waste much time.

JOHN

You had been gone for over a year.

CYNTHIA

Muses

A respectably, decent period, I suppose.

JOHN

Sounding a little stunned.

Respectably decent period for what?

CYNTHIA

Mourning, of course.

JOHN

Mourning? You are having a laugh Cyn.

CYNTHIA

No, not at all.

JOHN

But you just up and left without so much as a/

CYNTHIA

/I had a heart attack, John. It killed me stone dead. I didn't have much chance for an intimate farewell chat, not like when you buggered off to Hamburg.

JOHN

John appears saddened at this but reluctantly acknowledges the unscheduled manner of her departure...

So, you say.

CYNTHIA

Are you seeing George again?

JOHN

Yes, he's coming around tomorrow to pick up your chairs.

John points over in the direction of the two Ikea chairs and the "Thinking Chair."

CYNTHIA

Why?

JOHN

Because they're horrible, and he liked them.

CYNTHIA

I liked them.

JOHN

But you're not here now, so I can...

CYNTHIA

Cynthia flashes a withering expression with her lips pressed tightly together. She points over at the Ikea chairs again and moves her finger sideways to point at the "Thinking Chair."

That's interesting.

JOHN

Oh, do you think so? Everybody else thinks it is a pile of old shite.

CYNTHIA

Do they? I'm surprised.

Cynthia smirks

JOHN

Yes, they…

He glances at Cynthia and realises she is being sardonic.

CYNTHIA

It's a load of old crap, John. It looks like something Picasso might have knocked up on a day when he had severe constipation. You can be so gullible at times. Did you pay for it, or was it a gift?

JOHN

I liked it, so I bought it.

CYNTHIA

Did you?

JOHN

Yes, a lot.

CYNTHIA

You've been on your own for too long.

JOHN

John sneers gently

CYNTHIA

So, what is it supposed to be?

JOHN

John appears unsure as to whether Cynthia is really interested.

Are you sure you want to know?

CYNTHIA

Yes, go on, enlighten me; I'm intrigued.

JOHN

In a monotonic tenor.

Well, it's an existential facsimile of life. The artist is endeavouring to interpret the woefulness of the nihilistic world we inhabit and attempting to encapsulate that insight into a single object... a chair. The different angles and planes represent ethnicity, diverse cultures and religions. The pointy bits represent conflicting metaphysical opinions. It's called "The Thinking Chair."

CYNTHIA
The thinking chair?

JOHN
Yes.

CYNTHIA
Was it a nice shop?

JOHN
Curiously
Gallery actually.

CYNTHIA
A gallery… imposing...
Cynthia nods approvingly
beat
Did they offer you wine and cheesy nibbles?

JOHN
Yes, they did, actually.

CYNTHIA
That's nice.

JOHN
Yes, I thought so.

CYNTHIA
Did you meet the artist?

JOHN

Agnetha? Yes, I did, actually. She was very nice as well. I think she was Swedish or Norwegian. She explained how deep and meaningful the chair is and how it communicates with like-minded souls.

CYNTHIA

Was she a blonde with big tits by any chance?

JOHN

I can't remember.

CYNTHIA

Try.

JOHN

Are you supposed to ask me questions like that when you are de....?

John's voice fades away on the last word

CYNTHIA

Dead, John, that's all. You can say the word. You won't turn into a newt or anything. And, being dead doesn't stop me from being curious or from taking the piss.

JOHN

Oh, I see. It's just that I thought you would have risen above all that sort of stuff.

CYNTHIA

I have john; I'm just worried about you being alone.

JOHN

Oh.

CYNTHIA

So, John, did she have big tits?

JOHN

Abruptly

Yes… and she was a blonde.

CYNTHIA

Now I'm beginning to understand. So tell me all about the Spiky chair.

JOHN

Brusquely

It talks to me, more or less.

CYNTHIA

It talks to you?

JOHN

Yes! Sometimes.

CYNTHIA

Does it? Well, it still looks like a pile of old crap to me. I think you've been tucked up a treat.

JOHN

I knew you would say that. You can be so boringly pedestrian and dispassionate at times. I don't know why I bothered.

CYNTHIA

You know it's rubbish John, why don't you just admit it

JOHN

I like it.

CYNTHIA

How much did you pay for it?

JOHN

Two grand!

CYNTHIA

Cries loudly

Two thousand fucking pounds of my hard-earnt money wasted on that piece of shit? That's a grand for each tit.

JOHN

nonchalantly

Are angels allowed to swear?

CYNTHIA

Yes, we are. And I'm not a fucking angel John, I'm just dead.

JOHN
I'll remember that.

CYNTHIA
You should.

JOHN
I will.

CYNTHIA
You must have gone mad.

JOHN
Maybe, but anyway,
Pauses and then replies meekly.
It's not your money anymore; you left it all to me when you died.
John smirks

CYNTHIA
More fool me then. Should have left it to the donkeys.

JOHN
Bravado
But you didn't; you left it all to me.
John smirks again, and Cynthia shakes her head.

YONI
Yoni comes out of the bathroom
I do bedroom now, John.

JOHN

Okay.

YONI

Yoni notices the Thinking Chair.
That is nice John, is it new?

JOHN

Yes.

He waits contemplatively for her comment as she wanders around the Chair. Cynthia glances at John inquisitorially.

YONI

It's saying something to me John.

Cynthia tries not to laugh, and John awaits the denouncement he is sure is about to come.

CYNTHIA

Throw me on the fire.

Cynthia says this in a mockingly ghostly tone.
John flashes Cynthia an admonishing glance.

JOHN

Is it?

John asks cautiously while trying to ignore Cynthia's smirking.

YONI

It speaks to me of confusion and conflict… with just a tiny hint of chaos, and yet I feel compromise and resolution emanating from within - a sense of clarity…I feel the crescendo building as if a climactic moment of universal atonement has been achieved, and I sense the need to internalise through assimilation.

CYNTHIA

Cynthia falls off the sofa with laughter and mumbles
Fuck me.
John is stunned.
Yoni continues to stare at the chair.

JOHN

Yes…
Beat
John takes a deep breath.
Strangely… and you are not going to believe this, but that's precisely what it said to me when I first saw it.

CYNTHIA

Her mouth drops open in stunned disbelief.

YONI

I carry on in bedroom now Johnny.
She wanders off to the bedroom.

CYNTHIA

Gets up from the floor and sits back down on the sofa, still laughing.

Has to be your soulmate.

JOHN

She's my cleaner, that's it.

CYNTHIA

But you are both on the same planet; you're made for each other. I'm not sure which one that is mind you, probably the planet Zob... but you are definitely both on it.

JOHN

No. Absolutely not. That is never going to happen.

CYNTHIA

We'll see.

Lights go down - segue to next scene.

SCENE FIVE
One year later.

John's Flat.
Lucy is packing items into one of the many packing cases in the lounge.
John and Cynthia are sitting on the floor, both dressed in white.
The thinking Chair is still there.
The doorbell rings, Lucy answers.

LUCY

She smiles
> George.

GEORGE

> Lucy, I am so sorry to hear about John.

Lucy beckons George to come in.

LUCY

> You got my message?

GEORGE

> Yes, yes, I did… eventually. I'm sorry I didn't turn up at the funeral, I was away on holiday. I only got your message after I got back.

Lucy waves her hands as if to say, "no matter."

> So, when did he…

LUCY

Three weeks ago, the funeral was last week. Please sit down, if you can find somewhere. I'm sorry it's a bit of a mess,

beat

I'm packing everything up ready for the charity shop.

John glances over, looking appalled.

Would you like a cup of tea?

GEORGE

Only if you're making one.

LUCY

I am. I've been at it for hours. I could do with a break.

Lucy crosses to the kitchen to make tea.

GEORGE

Did many people come?

LUCY

Only a few. He would never have wanted a fuss. Julian, Yoni and I went, and a few people from the publishers turned up, some people I didn't know… oh and Pauli came with his wife.

GEORGE

Sounding surprised

Did he?

LUCY

He was nice. Even said a few words

JOHN

To Cynthia sounding surprised
Did he?

CYNTHIA

Yes, I did mention it last week.

JOHN

Did you?

CYNTHIA

Cynthia nods
Yes… He must have forgiven you at last.

JOHN

So it would seem.

CYNTHIA

You should have come… it was great fun.

JOHN

I'm not sure about the fun bit, and anyway, I was there in a manner of speaking.

CYNTHIA

Flashes an expression of incredulity.
That doesn't count.

JOHN

Did you?

CYNTHIA

What?

JOHN

Go to yours.

CYNTHIA

Yes.

JOHN

John Shrugs

Na didn't fancy it much. It would have been a bit odd standing around listening to people I can't recall telling nice little stories about me that I'd rather forget or can't remember anymore.

CYNTHIA

Most people I know go along to theirs... out of curiosity more than anything else. There's not much else to do around here, and it is a nice day out.

JOHN

Startled.

A nice day out, for fucks sake?
I could think of better things to do than furtively loitering around my own funeral listening to banal inanities and clichéd eulogies.

CYNTHIA

And anyway, how do you know they would have said nice things? I would have said you were an absolute bastard; in fact, I did mention it once or twice.

JOHN

John smiles smugly.

But you weren't really there, so you couldn't.

CYNTHIA

I was there actually, just couldn't say anything... well, I did say something, but no one could hear me. I stood alongside the vicar making funny faces and slipping in the odd comment.

Beat.

JOHN

Did they?

CYNTHIA

What?

JOHN

Say nice things about me.

CYNTHIA

Appearing surprised at John's concern.

Do you really care?

JOHN

Of course I care; that's my legacy...

CYNTHIA

Acerbically

Your legacy! What is?

JOHN

The things I did. My creations are what people will remember me for and what I leave to posterity: it's my heritage and my legacy.

CYNTHIA

Cynthia steels herself from laughing, stunned by Johns spectacular arrogance
But you never did anything apart from a few iffy doodles in my books.

JOHN

Sounding offended by the demeaning slight
Iffy doodles?

CYNTHIA

Yes. Doodles.

JOHN

That was a bit hurtful; I did try.

CYNTHIA

Smugly and with a smirk.
No prizes for trying.

JOHN

Grunts and takes a swig from a glass of whiskey he is holding.

CYNTHIA

beat
They did, actually.

JOHN

What?

Appearing confused

CYNTHIA

At your funeral - say some nice things... I thought I was at the wrong one for a moment.

JOHN

Smiles

You do make me laugh, even if you are a little wounding at times.

CYNTHIA

So, I do still make you laugh?

JOHN

Yes

CYNTHIA

That's good,

JOHN

Is it?

CYNTHIA

It's very precious; you can't buy that sort of chemistry. It comes with time... being together.

JOHN

John muses on that comment for a few seconds

Most of them were probably fibbing... a little.
It's colouring between the lines...
People bend the truth at funerals, forget the bad
bits and start thinking about their own
mortality. That makes them say nice things.
In reality, their vapid platitudes... are driven by
self-concern... fear of the unknown.

CYNTHIA

You are an old cynic; you're worse than me at
times.

JOHN

Am I?

CYNTHIA

Yes.

JOHN

Anyway, we're together now, that's all that
matters.

CYNTHIA

Fuck me, are you going soft in the head as
we've got older or have you had a joint?

JOHN

No, I mean it, and we can't be getting older.
We're dead... forever, but always the same age.

John smirks

CYNTHIA

So we are John… so we are, I almost forgot.
Cynthia takes a sip of her tea.

LUCY TO GEORGE

John wanted you to have his guitar. He left a sticky note stuck on his Will.

CYNTHIA

That was nice.

JOHN

I'm a nice bloke.

CYNTHIA

In your dreams.

GEORGE

I was banking on getting the spiky chair.
George points at The Thinking Chair mockingly.
Lucy Smiles

JOHN

He's taking the piss; I should have left him my bag of piss instead.
He pats the position on his hip where his stoma bag would have been.

CYNTHIA

Not such a nice bloke now.

JOHN

John scoffs at Cynthia's comment

LUCY TO GEORGE

A little surprised.

Oh, were you, I could have a word with Yoni, he left it to her with a rather strange letter…

GEORGE

No, I was only joking. I told him it was a piece of old crap, and he got pretty upset, as I remember. I was always chiding him over the chair. I would love to have the guitar. I never understood the chair.

LUCY

Nobody did except Yoni.

CYNTHIA

It really was a piece of old crap.

JOHN

It was a valuable piece of art.

CYNTHIA

Art my arse, Blondie big tits saw you coming…
beat
So, you left it to Yoni?
Cynthia says this with an interrogatory questioning smirk

JOHN

Nonplussed
Yes.

CYNTHIA

Looking at John suspiciously
Did you have sex with her?

JOHN

Guardedly
Why do you ask?

CYNTHIA

I don't know, not really my business, I suppose,
I just wondered, that's all.

JOHN

I don't know if I should answer the question?

CYNTHIA

You have…you just did.

JOHN

Alright, we did have a relationship.

CYNTHIA

A little sternly
I knew it. After I died, I hope?

JOHN

A little taken back by the question
Yes… of course. It was after Jane buggered off.
beat
Didn't last though, the cleaning began to suffer,
so I kicked her into touch, but she carried on
with the cleaning…

CYNTHIA

Laughs
And she stayed.

JOHN

Of course she did; it was only a shag or two and the occasional blow job.

CYNTHIA

Eaaa.
Pretends to vomit
Too much information.

JOHN

We did have some synergy, and there is… was my magnetic charm.

CYNTHIA

Smiles
Strange that… I never noticed.

JOHN

Sounding a little alarmed
Were you watching us?

CYNTHIA

Of course, it was good for a laugh. As I said, there's not much else to do around here.
Cynthia scrunches up her nose.
beat
You do have some very cheesy lines John… You'd never have got away with them with me.

JOHN

That is just so weird… what else did you see?

CYNTHIA

Makes another throwing up gesture while poking her fingers down her throat.

I watched you propose to her; I nearly threw up.

JOHN

You asked me just now if I had an affair, but you must have known all along if you were watching me.

CYNTHIA

Just testing, and we didn't watch you all the time, we couldn't stomach some of it

JOHN

She said she didn't think the time was quite right, but she would give it some deep and meaningful consideration.

CYNTHIA

She actually said you were a fat twat and a bit desperate, so she gave you a couple of sympathy fucks. Then she told you to get a life.

JOHN

You heard?

CYNTHIA

Yes… of course I heard that bit. I almost pissed myself

JOHN

You shouldn't have been watching; it was an intimate moment between the two of us.

CYNTHIA

Seven of us, actually.

JOHN

Seven, what the fuck, why seven?

CYNTHIA

There was nothing decent on Netflix, so I had some of our old friends around, and we had a few beers and pizzas. I told them it would be a good laugh… and it was. We all made lots of witty comments and got pissed. You would have laughed your head off.

JOHN

John is flabbergasted

A few friends taking the piss out of me was that all my life amounted to in the end?

CYNTHIA

She tilts her head to one side and smirks
beat.

You did have another one you know, one that would have ended quite differently?

JOHN

Another life? What do you mean?

CYNTHIA

Just that. Another life, the one you would have had if you hadn't had the one you had.

JOHN

What the fuck does that mean.

CYNTHIA

Have you not spoken to Brian yet? He's in charge of the O.L.D.

JOHN

The O.L.D.?

CYNTHIA

The Other Life Department. Everybody has two possible lives. The one you would have had, and the one you had, the one you get is down to destiny,   a flip of a coin usually, one tiny change in circumstances and….

JOHN

And what was mine.

CYNTHIA

Do you really want to know? You can't go back and change it now, so what's the point?

JOHN

persistently
    Do you know?

CYNTHIA

What your other life could have been like?

JOHN

Yes.

CYNTHIA

Yes, I had a look. I was bored one Wednesday it was raining so... but I wasn't going to mention it.

JOHN

So what's the point in telling me you know what you know if you are not going to tell me what you know? That's just some sick manifestation of purgatory... I thought it was the other lot that dispensed the philosophical horse shit.

John points downwards with a scrunched up facial expression

CYNTHIA

Cynthia muses for a few moments
Well, it's not much, really.

JOHN

Irritated
Not much?

CYNTHIA

Well, you would have been famous, that's all.

JOHN

Exclaims vociferously
Famous? How fucking famous?

CYNTHIA

Does it matter now?

JOHN

Exasperatedly
Of course, it matters.

CYNTHIA

Well, it all goes back to when you nearly got that recording contract with the bloke at Decca... what was his name?

JOHN

Rowe...Dick Rowe, how can I forget him?

CYNTHIA

Yes, that was his name; any way you didn't get it, he rejected you and the band. He said he couldn't see groups making a comeback. Cliff and the Shadows had that market all sewn up.

JOHN

John is stunned.
Yea, I know that much... I was there.

CYNTHIA

Well, that's when it could all have changed... Brian Epstein came to see you, and he liked you.

JOHN

Eppy liked us?

CYNTHIA

Well, he was quite taken with you; thought you had a pert little arse, but yes, he liked the whole band, and he signed you up, and you became world-famous, and you made a lot of money. That's it.

JOHN

Famous! That would have been brilliant.

CYNTHIA

Well, not actually, just nearly Famous.

JOHN

That would have still been brilliant!

CYNTHIA

Well, not really, not for me anyway.

JOHN

Why?

CYNTHIA

Well, in your Other Life, you dumped me and married some Japanese bint.

JOHN

I'd never do that.

CYNTHIA
John, you did… in your other life.

JOHN
Looking a little sheepish.
Oh, I'm sorry.

CYNTHIA
Nothing to be sorry about; it never happened.

JOHN
Oh no, of course not……
Long pause…..
but if we had been famous?

CYNTHIA
Cynthia is expecting this question
Yes?

JOHN
Just how famous were we?

CYNTHIA
You became the most famous band the world has ever seen.

JOHN
But how famous is that?

CYNTHIA
Does it matter now?

JOHN

Of course it matters.

CYNTHIA

The girls screamed louder than they did for Elvis

JOHN

Louder than the king?

CYNTHIA

Yes.

JOHN

Louder than Cliff?

CYNTHIA

Yes, much louder, so loud no one could hear you playing.

JOHN

That loud. Probably not a bad thing.

CYNTHIA

Why?

JOHN

Well, we did have off days.

CYNTHIA

The great John Lennon had an off day?

JOHN

Not just me, everybody, we were fucked in Hamburg, most of the time, so Christ knows, oops; sorry, but Christ knows what it would have been like if nobody could hear us.

CYNTHIA

Well, you managed to make twelve albums, so not too shabby.

JOHN

Twelve! You're having a fucking laugh.

CYNTHIA

You managed to make it to 1970 before you broke up. You would have sold over a hundred and fifty million albums to date. And the number would still be climbing.

JOHN

Bugger me.

CYNTHIA

Laughs

More than any other artist, ever.

JOHN

Fuck!

CYNTHIA

And then you all started making solo albums

JOHN

What even George the Sky guy?

CYNTHIA

Yes, George and even Ringo.

JOHN

Aah, Now I know you're taking the piss; he wasn't even in the band.

CYNTHIA

Oh, but he was. He joined in 1963, just before it all kicked off. Eppy suggested it.

JOHN

Oh Christ, did I have to let him fuck me?

CYNTHIA

Well, the jury's still out on that, but you were definitely very friendly, you know what I mean
Cynthia laughs.
I'm sure you would have enjoyed it?
Another quirky searching smile

JOHN

I'm glad Ringo joined. That was good. I liked him. Pete was rubbish even if he was my best mate.

CYNTHIA

The world loved him.

JOHN

More than me?

CYNTHIA

Give me a break John.

JOHN

Who was the Japanese bint?

CYNTHIA

Yoko was her name. She was an artist.

JOHN

That sounds about right. Shame I didn't take the other life.

CYNTHIA

Well, thanks for that.

JOHN

Only joking Cyn.

CYNTHIA

Throws John a doubtful expression.

JOHN

So it all turned out well in the end?

CYNTHIA

Not quite.

JOHN

Not quite; I don't like the sound of that.

CYNTHIA

There was one other thing.

JOHN

What? More?

CYNTHIA

You didn't make it to seventy-one.

JOHN

Didn't make it, but I was famous?

CYNTHIA

Famous, yes. But dead... very dead.

JOHN

Stunned
> Dead?

CYNTHIA

Yes, shot dead by a loony in Manhattan...

JOHN

Manhattan in New York?

CYNTHIA

I don't think there's one in Bognor.

JOHN

Still staggered.
> Dead?

CYNTHIA

Yes. When you were forty.

JOHN

Fuck me... not much of a life.

CYNTHIA

Oh, I think you had a good other life, just a little short.

JOHN

But I got this one instead?

CYNTHIA

You're getting the idea now, and this one was a lot longer.

JOHN

Oh.

CYNTHIA

So, what do you think?

JOHN

Think? I don't know; it's a lot to take in.

CYNTHIA

As I see it, in the end, you're either dead, or you're dead. The only difference is time; nothing else really matters. You can't take the money or the fame with you.

JOHN

Hmm

John and Cynthia sit back and listen to George and Lucy.

GEORGE

wistfully

So, I guess that's the end of everything now.

LUCY

The end?

GEORGE

When I last spoke to John, we talked about the old days, when we were in the band and how we would be famous one day... the four of us. We were going to arrange some sort of reunion.

John looks at Cynthia

Cynthia holds both her hands out palms upwards and makes a tight-lipped smiley expression.

JOHN TO CYNTHIA

He doesn't know about the Other Life...?

CYNTHIA

Not yet.

LUCY TO GEORGE

That would have been nice.

GEORGE

Yes, it would. Still in another life now, hey?

LUCY

Do you ever think back to what might have been?

GEORGE

Anybody who has ever been in a band does that. Those that never make it that is. You always wonder about the life you would have had...

JOHN

John glances at Cynthia and exclaims.
Or could have had!

LUCY

Still, you had a good life, didn't you George?

GEORGE

I can't complain... well, I could...
But nobody would listen.
George chuckles to himself.
I don't know if anybody ever really listens when you talk about your feelings; I mean... why would they care.

LUCY

If they loved you, they would care.

GEORGE

Maybe.

There's a knock at the door, and Lucy walks over to open it, and Yoni is standing there.

YONI
Hello Miss Lucy, how are you?

LUCY
I'm fine, Yoni, come in.

YONI
On seeing all the boxes, she light-heartedly comments,
Oh! You do my job; you put me out of business!

LUCY
Slightly embarrassed.
No, I am just packing up dad's things, getting ready to take them to the charity shop.

YONI
Yoni smiles at George
Hello Mr Skyman.

GEORGE
Appears intrigued
Mr Skyman?

YONI
Yes, John, he talks about you all the time, he say you fix Sky, but he says you are also really good friend from many years ago.

GEORGE

Oh, I see.

YONI

To Lucy

Yes, I understand. I was only jesting. It must be done, I know. When the present is over, and there is no future, we must tidy the past. One cannot step twice into the same water in a river.

LUCY

Lucy smiles, a little puzzled by Yoni's aphorism.

Yes, I suppose you're right, Yoni… where did you read that, in a Christmas cracker.

Not said disparagingly

YONI

Looking perplexed

No, why would I read that in Christmas cracker? I am not an imbecile.

Very firmly

That is Nietzsche!

LUCY

Apologetically

Oop's my apologies. Anyway, the reason I rang you is because John left you something in his will.

YONI

No apology needed; I did read in Christmas cracker, not Nietzsche. I blame John; he tries to teach me about sardonic irony. I not always get it right.

LUCY

That's dad.

YONI

I bet he left me hoover. Johnny very naughty at times.

LUCY

Smiles

Was he?

A little surprised.

No, Yoni, not the hoover. He left you that.

Lucy points at The Thinking Chair.

He said you talked about it many times and that you…

Lucy takes a note from out of her pocket and quotes,

"believed it encompassed the existential affectation of life, the artist's interpretation of the nihilistic world encapsulated in a single object, the soul of eternity."

YONI

No… I was only joking with Johnny. He liked to take piss, you know, it's just a load of old crap. I would throw it on the fire if I was you. Nobody want it.

Lucy appears flummoxed by Yoni's answer.

LUCY

Oh, I see. Well, in that case, I think you've had a wasted journey.

YONI

It's no problem. I like coming here for last time. Many happy memories.

LUCY

Yes, dad did mention something about…

YONI

Oh, you talk about when he fuck me, yes?

LUCY

Embarrassed again.

Well, not exactly, but he did mention you had a romantic fling. So I thought you should have something as a keepsake.

YONI

Lucy… I have my memory of lovely days; that is all I need, thank you. I don't need things thank you. It's not as if he were really famous, then it might be different… I could sell stuff for lots of money and be rich.. but he not famous, so I not get rich, but nothing get spoilt, and I am always happy. Johnny always sing me song when I am sad, and that will last forever.

Yoni smiles at Lucy

LUCY
Oh, did he? What song was that?

YONI
I see you in my Dreams.

GEORGE
I always liked that song.

LUCY
Oh yes, he always sang that one to me when I was a little girl to get me to sleep when I went to bed.

GEORGE
I could sing it for you if you like? One last time before we leave.

Lucy and Yoni nod. George picks up a ukulele.

JOHN
Oh, for Christ's sake.

CYNTHIA
Shut up John, it's a lovely song; you used to sing it to me when I was sad.

JOHN
Did I?

George starts to play

Lonely days are long
Twilight sings a song
All the happiness that used to be

Soon my eyes will close
Soon I'll find repose
And in dreams
You're always near to me

I'll see you in my dreams
Hold you in my dreams
Someone took you out of my arms
Still, I feel the thrill of your charms

Lips that once were mine
Tender eyes that shine
They will light my way tonight
I'll see you in my dreams

JOHN

Did I really sing it to you?
Cynthia smiles at John

CYNTHIA

Yes, long ago when I was sad, and I'm a little
sad now

JOHN

Are you?

CYNTHIA

Just a little,

JOHN

Why?

CYNTHIA

Because it's all over John... forever.

JOHN

Well, if Hamilton shuts up for a moment, I could sing the song for you.

John picks up a ukulele and joins in with George.

Lips that once were mine
Tender eyes that shine
They will light my way tonight
I'll see you in my dreams

They will light my lonely way tonight
I'll see you in my dreams

Reprise.
Lights fade

Then engage the audience for one last chorus with all the cast.

THE END

Printed in Great Britain
by Amazon

69460592R00098